STRENGTH
for the Journey

```
Power for Living a Victorious Christian Life
       ~A 21-day Inspirational Devotional~
```

Mary A. Ford

Unless otherwise noted, all scripture is taken from the New King James Version®. Copyright © 1982 by Thomas Nelson. Used by permission. All rights reserved.

Scripture quotations marked (AMP) are taken from the Amplified Bible, Copyright © 1954, 1958, 1962, 1964, 1965, 1987 by The Lockman Foundation. Used by permission.

Scripture quotations marked (ASV) are taken from the American Standard Version of the Bible. Copyright 1901, Thomas Nelson, now in public domain.

Scripture quotations marked (ERV) are taken from the HOLY BIBLE: EASY-TO-READ VERSION © 2001 by World Bible Translation Center, Inc. and used by permission.

Scripture quotations marked ESV are from The ESV® Bible (The Holy Bible, English Standard Version®), copyright © 2001 by Crossway, a publishing ministry of Good News Publishers. Used by permission. All rights reserved.

Scriptures marked GW are taken from the GOD'S WORD (GW): Scripture taken from GOD'S WORD® copyright© 1995 by God's Word to the Nations. All rights reserved.

Scripture quotations marked NASB are taken from the New American Standard Bible® (NASB), Copyright © 1960, 1962, 1963, 1968, 1971, 1972, 1973, 1975, 1977, 1995 by The Lockman Foundation Used by permission. www.Lockman.org

Scripture quotations marked (NIV) are taken from the Holy Bible, New International Version®, NIV®. Copyright © 1973, 1978, 1984, 2011 by Biblica, Inc.™ Used by permission of Zondervan. All rights reserved worldwide. www.zondervan.com The "NIV" and "New International Version" are trademarks registered in the United States Patent and Trademark Office by Biblica, Inc.™

Scripture quotations marked (NLT) are taken from the Holy Bible, New Living Translation, copyright ©1996, 2004, 2015 by Tyndale House Foundation. Used by permission of Tyndale House Publishers, a Division of Tyndale House Ministries, Carol Stream, Illinois 60188. All rights reserved.

Copyright © 2019 Mary A. Ford

www.duty2delightministries.com

All rights reserved. No part of this book may be reproduced in any form or by any electronic or mechanical means without permission in writing from the author or publisher, except as allowed under USA copyright laws.

Cover design by Radical Women

Publisher: bylisabell
Radical Women
(DBA)
PO Box 782
Granbury, TX
76048
www.bylisabell.com

ISBN: 978-1-7340398-2-5

DEDICATION

STRENGTH for The Journey *is dedicated to my beloved siblings –* **Debra and Leon**

May you both continue to find joy, peace, encouragement and STRENGTH in Christ as you unfold each day of your life's journey!
Love Eternally ~ Mary

Contents

Special Features	vii
Introduction	1
Day One: STRENGTH for the Journey	3
Day Two: With God — It is Possible	11
Day Three: Lord, Why Me?	16
Day Four: The Joy of the Lord is Your STRENGTH	21
Day Five: Is Your BUT Bigger Than Your God?	26
Day Six: Somebody Bigger	31
Day Seven: God is Our Refuge and STRENGTH	37
Day Eight: Such as I Have	43
Day Nine: Lord, STRENGTHEN My Hands	48
Day Ten: Speak No Evil	52
Day Eleven: What's in a Name?	57
Day Twelve: Ministry Matters	63
Day Thirteen: Seeking God First	68
Day Fourteen: Seasons of Sorrows	72
Day Fifteen: He Will Do It!	76
Day Sixteen: Spiritual Physique	81
Day Seventeen: Fear or Faith?	87
Day Eighteen: Lord, Make Me Over!	93
Day Nineteen: Armed & Dangerous	98
Day Twenty: The Belly of the Beast	104
Day Twenty-one: STRENGTH for the Believer	109
ABOUT THE AUTHOR	114
Other Books by Mary A. Ford	116
Mary's Most Popular Prayer Classes and Workshops	117

Special Features

This devotional contains the following special features to help stimulate a deeper personal experience as you spend dedicated time with God each day during your 21-day journey.

❖ *"Focus Scriptures"* that relate to the topic of the day begins each devotional.

❖ *"Think About It"* is a composite of concepts, thoughts, scriptures and questions following each devotional. The purpose is to help the believer reflect on ways to apply biblical truths, mature spiritually, and grow from life's lessons.

❖ *"Time With God Prayer"* is designed to guide the believer into focused prayer that addresses life challenges, which can often hinder the Christian walk. This section begins with a prayer by the author, revolving around selected scripture and the topic of the day. Space is provided for the reader to complete the prayer with personal thoughts, desires, intercessions, petitions, thanksgiving and praises to the Lord.

Introduction

I love to unwrap gifts! Although receiving the actual gift is exciting, I still find exceeding joy in unwrapping a gift—so, I make a really big deal out of the experience! I never just rip off the wrapping paper to get to the gift inside more quickly. Rather, I take my time—slowly and carefully removing the bow and then the outer paper. I express my appreciation of the gift wrapping talents of the gift-giver and rave over the time it took to nicely wrap a gift just for me. The anticipation then mounts as the final piece of tape is removed, and the wrapping paper slips away from the box. I quickly open the box to reveal the special gift inside. You see, for me, it's not just about *"the gift."* My joy comes from the entire experience—*the journey*!

Life is a special gift from God just waiting to be unwrapped, embraced and enjoyed each day—regardless of the trials we may encounter along the way. As we travel the road of life—all while looking forward to spending eternity in heaven—we must always remember that our *journey* (earthly daily living) is just as important as our *destination* (eternal heavenly life). Yes—Jesus wants us to have that abundant life here on earth that He spoke about in John 10:10. *"I have come that they may have life, and that they may have it more abundantly."*

Each devotional contained in this book is designed to inspire spiritual growth and cultivate a deeper intimacy with Christ. Therefore, for the next 21 days, consider each day a *gift* from the Lord. Slowly *unwrap* each day by spending dedicated time in His presence through prayer and the study of His Word. Allow this special time spent daily with the Lord to help prune, prepare and transform you into a priceless original design created to be used for God's glory—on earth and in heaven!

I encourage you to take whatever time is necessary as you unwrap each daily devotional, allowing the scriptures, lessons, principles and prayers to penetrate your heart, saturate your soul, and transform your mind and heart. Meditate upon each focus scripture and recite the support scriptures throughout the day, allowing the Holy Spirit to speak to you on a personal and intimate level.

As you apply God's principles to your daily living, and spend more and more dedicated time each day in His presence, you will find yourself leaning less to your own understanding, casting aside worldly ways and standing firmly on God's promises in times of temptation, trials or triumphs. You will experience life in a new light each day as you tap into the *STRENGTH* you need for *The Journey*!

Mary A. Ford

Day One
STRENGTH for the Journey

He gives power to the weak, and to those who have no might He increases strength. Even the youths shall faint and be weary, and the young men shall utterly fall, but those who wait on the LORD Shall renew their STRENGTH (Isaiah 40:29-31).

God has called each one of us to travel a road that is not promised to always be smooth. This road is called LIFE. As we travel life's road, oftentimes, we run into roadblocks of bad marriages, ditches of dysfunctional relationships, fatally fractured finances and even hazardous health conditions. Not to mention devastating detours taken as a result of falling into potholes of worldly pleasures.

These life experiences can cause the believer to burn out, give up and even throw in the towel. But take heart. Even when you experience such setbacks and adversity along life's way, which can cause your journey to be difficult at best, Jesus still wants you to experience that abundant life He spoke about in John 10:10, *"I have come that they may have life, and that they may have it more abundantly."* The believer can take comfort in knowing that God's Word contains exactly what is needed to help uplift the downcast, refresh the faint and weary, restore the damaged and depleted, and provide *STRENGTH* for The Journey!

To help you grow stronger, persevere in life, and experience the *"joy of the Lord,"* which transcends happiness, I present for personal application during the next 21 days the following eight (8) steps in the form of an acrostic—using each letter in the word STRENGTH.

Step #1—[S] Study the Word
It is vitally important to study God's Word regularly. The Word is God's blueprint for living victoriously. As you encounter daily challenges, obstacles and pains, retreat to God's Word for direction, insight and inspiration. God's Word is like a light—it will brighten up your dark days. God's Word is like a GPS—it will guide you through life's difficult situations. God's Word is like a hammer—it will crush and destroy any weapon formed against you.! God's Word is like an anchor—it will hold and keep you rooted and grounded through any storm of life. *Meditate on Psalm 119:97-105.*

Step #2—[T] Trust God's Heart
Even when you don't understand what God is doing in your life, know that you can trust God's heart—the essence of who God is. His unconditional love for you and His character will never change or fail, regardless of your life season, because of who He is—merciful, patient, kind, righteous, slow to anger, forgiving, faithful and abundant in His love for you. God never gives up on you, and His love never runs out. No matter what you may be going through, trust God! *Meditate on Proverbs 3:5-8; Psalm 103:8.*

Step #3—[R] Rest in Jesus
Life's journey can sometimes leave you physically, mentally, emotionally and spiritually drained and exhausted. Learn how and when to REST. God promises to renew the weary one who waits and rests in Him. When you rest in God, He will exchange your human strength for His supernatural strength. In God's strength, you can not only survive but

thrive on your journey! *Meditate on 1 Kings 19:5-8; Psalm 73:25-26; Isaiah 40:31.*

Step #4 – [E] Evaluate Yourself

Perform self-evaluations – often! Assess anything in your life that may be draining you physically, mentally and emotionally. Perhaps even weighing you down spiritually – causing a disconnect from God or possibly hindering your Christian walk. Nothing can be off-limits to evaluate – relationships, work, hobbies, and even your ministry. Look at your hurts, habits and your hang-ups. When and where needed, confess, repent and make adjustments according to God's Word. God will give you a clean heart and a clean life. *Meditate on Psalm 139:23-24; Psalm 51:1-10.*

Step #5 – [N] Never Stop Praying

Pray without ceasing! Prayer should not be something believers do only in fight or flight situations. Prayer is an intricate part of the believer's intimate relationship with the Father. Prayer is a divine power that is rooted and grounded in God's omnipotence – not your own! Prayer allows one to step out of time and into eternity, where all things become possible. In order to have strength for the journey, you must stay connected in prayer to the main power source, which is God Himself. *Meditate on Ephesians 6:18; Matthew 19:26; 1 Thessalonians 5:16-18.*

Step #6 – [G] Give it Over to Jesus

Understand that you cannot bear life's burdens alone – nor were you ever meant to. Jesus promised to be your burden bearer and heavy load sharer. Accept the fact that you can't fix everything. Jesus alone has the strength to carry all burdens, and He alone can bear all pain. Learn to surrender your problems, pains and woes, turning them all over to Jesus. He can fix it—whatever "it" looks like. *Meditate on Matthew 11:28-30.*

Step #7 — [T] Thank God "IN" ALL Things

Even when you can't thank God "for" the difficult times, you can still thank God "in" difficult times. Recall what God has done for you in the past. Instead of having a pity party for your current situation, try having a praise party for your past blessings and victories. Tap into your strength as a believer by cultivating an attitude of gratitude. Every time you think, thank Him. *Meditate on Psalm 100:3-5.*

Step #8 — [H] Hallelujah! — Always Give GOD Praise!

Hallelujah! This word has a universal meaning around the world, and it is the highest acclamation of praise God can receive in heaven and on earth. Seek to praise God for who He is—not just thank Him for what He does for you. Ask God to help you get your focus right so you can see clearly who He is—even in the midst of dire situations. Once your focus is on the omnipotent, omnipresent, omniscience, sovereign God, then you can give Him the highest praise. Hallelujah! *Meditate on Psalm 150.*

This page intentionally left blank.

~*THINK ABOUT IT*~

The previous eight (8) steps are essential to weathering life's storms and to having a healthy spiritual lifestyle that produces good fruit. When put into daily practice, they will help fortify your faith, strengthen spiritual resolve, and promote abundant living.

Humbly and honestly think about your life right now. How do you measure up in each of these eight areas? In what area(s) might you need to improve? What changes are you willing to make?

Write down on the lines below your answers to the previous questions, and your desires and plans to apply these eight steps in your life during the next 21 days.

_____
_____
_____
_____
_____
_____
_____
_____
_____
_____
_____
_____
_____
_____
_____
_____

Time With God Prayer

Heavenly Father – Oh, how worthy you are of worship! All honor, praise and glory belong to you alone. As your children begin this 21-day journey, help them fully and completely commit themselves to you – mind, body and soul. Father, open eyes so they might see you clearly. Open ears so they might hear your still, small voice as you speak gently to them each day. Circumcise hearts so your loving presence is felt, embraced and enjoyed. Free minds so that worshipping you becomes a lifestyle choice expressed in spirit and truth each day. It's in the strong and mighty name of Jesus I pray, Amen.

Meditate on Psalm 19:14. Writeced out your personal prayer for STRENGTH below.

_____
_____
_____
_____
_____
_____
_____
_____
_____
_____
_____
_____
_____
_____
_____

In Jesus' name, I pray, Amen

This page intentionally left blank.

Day Two
With God—It is Possible

Come, let us rebuild the wall of Jerusalem. Then we will not be ashamed anymore (Nehemiah 2:17, ERV).

One day, the prophet Nehemiah received a visit from his brother, Hanani, and some other friends who sojourned to Susa from Judah. As they greeted one another with holy hugs and kisses, Nehemiah eagerly inquired about his fellow Jewish brethren who escaped Babylonian captivity and remained in Judah. With equal anticipation, he also inquired about the city of Jerusalem. But as his brother began to share with him the dismal emotional state of the Jewish people and the broken condition of the city of Jerusalem, Nehemiah began to weep bitterly. As he listened to tales of his people living in shame because of the shattered city walls and burned gates, Nehemiah was so disturbed that he fasted and prayed for several days as his heart longed to return home and rebuild the city walls and gates of Jerusalem (Nehemiah 1:1-4, 11, 2:1-9).

Needless to say, this was not an easy task Nehemiah was about to undertake. Jerusalem was in a pile of ruins. Its gates had been burned to the ground, and the people were displaced and depressed. I'm sure that after talking to some of the people, inspecting the city, and assessing the tremendous damage, most people would have felt overwhelmed and would begin having second thoughts, thinking "I've bitten off more than I can chew!" But, not

Nehemiah. He boldly proclaimed to the Israelites, *"with God, it is possible."*

Like Nehemiah, what walls in your life are yet in ruin? What devastating, damaged or estranged condition might your life seem to be in at this present moment in time? Is there some area in your physical, emotional or spiritual world causing you shame and unrest? Perhaps you have tried time and time again to resolve a reoccurring issue, or maybe defeat a giant in your life that just won't fall!

No, this was definitely not an easy task for Nehemiah, and it will by no means be an easy task for you. I'm sure, at times, Nehemiah and his co-laborers felt weak, afraid, and they didn't know how they could go on to complete the needed work under such great opposition from their enemies. Where would they get STRENGTH to complete what they started? But, despite overwhelming odds, they refused to give up. Nehemiah remained steadfast in prayer, seeking God's divine guidance while he took every counter action he could in order to stay one step ahead of his enemies and complete His God-ordained task (Nehemiah 6:1-15).

You, too, can do the same! First—pray fervently, passionately and persistently about those areas of your life you've identified as *"needing repairs."* Nehemiah prayed passionately and fervently to God, confessing and asking forgiveness of Israel's sins while imploring God to extend His abundant mercy toward His chosen people. As you seek God in prayer, remember your family, friends and others in your life that may need your prayers of intercession along the way.

Secondly, don't hesitate to add a time of *fasting* to your quest in order to accomplish the *impossible* through Christ! Nehemiah humbly reminded God of His promises, persisted in prayer, and asked the Father for favor with those in authority to have everything he needed to accomplish his task. Through prayer, coupled with fasting, God moved upon the hearts of both the king and queen, resulting in the provision of everything needed for Nehemiah's success (Nehemiah 1:11, 2:1-9).

Lastly, as you step out on faith into this 21-day life-changing journey, just as God was with Nehemiah, remember, *He will also be with you!* And He will give you *STRENGTH for the journey.*

~THINK ABOUT IT~

What extreme actions are you willing to take in order to right the wrongs, rebuild relationships, refresh your faith, renew your walk with Christ, or mend the damaged areas of your life? God will strengthen you to endure and overcome whatever trials, tasks, temptations or challenges set before you.

Write down on the lines below those things in your life that appear to be holding you back from being and accomplishing everything God has planned for you. Write down anything hindering you from reaching the plans and promises of God—*Jeremiah 29:11*.

_____
_____
_____
_____
_____
_____
_____
_____
_____
_____
_____
_____
_____
_____
_____
_____
_____
_____

Time With God Prayer

Heavenly Father, help your children to have the fortitude, tenacity, courage and faith of Nehemiah. No matter what they may face or what may be facing them, help them to stand strong and firm in their faith as they trust you to do the impossible! It's in the powerful and matchless name of Jesus I humbly pray – Amen.

Meditate on Psalm 46:1. Write out your personal prayer for STRENGTH to do the IMPOSSIBLE.

_____
_____
_____
_____
_____
_____
_____
_____
_____
_____
_____
_____
_____
_____
_____
_____
_____
_____
_____

In Jesus' name, I pray, Amen.

Day Three
Lord, Why Me?

But as for me, my feet had almost stumbled; my steps had nearly slipped…Until I went into the sanctuary of God; Then I understood their end…But it is good for me to draw near to God; I have put my trust in the Lord GOD, that I may declare all Your works (Psalm 73:2, 17, 28).

Asaph, the writer of the 73rd Psalm, leads us on his journey of emotions as he ponders the sight of the wicked all around him. He begins by acknowledging the goodness of the Lord to those who have a pure heart, but then he swiftly transitions into a period of confession—acknowledging how he almost lost his balance and slipped into sin because of the injustices of the wicked he constantly saw as he strived to live a life of holiness.

Perhaps, as you strive to live righteously, you too have found your physical and spiritual strength failing as your eyes wonder in amazement at the prosperity of the wicked. Your desire to live holy is very much intact, but you find your faith flooded with doubts of whether you will have the strength to endure the swift transitions of life.

Well, you are not alone. Overwhelmed by the arrogant pride, extravagant spending, the cruel dominance, and never-ending prosperity of the wicked, the Psalmist poured out his heart in confession and complaint before his sovereign savior. He indeed had a spiritual battle going on within himself—he was green with envy and jealousy.

But in the midst of all his complaining, pouting, and self-pity, he finally found his way into the house of the Lord. There in the house of prayer and the presence of the Lord, he was given divine revelation of his own sinful nature, the tragedy of the wicked, and the blessedness of trusting in God. It was while he worshiped that his complaints turned into prayers of praise and hope, leaving him with a testimony of God's goodness, love, protection and provision. *"But it is good for me to draw near to God; I have put my trust in the Lord GOD, that I may declare all your works."* (Psalm 73:28)

MORAL TO THE STORY: If you expect to defeat the enemy—*from without and within*—then stop looking *out* at others and start looking *up* to God for the STRENGTH needed not only to survive tough times but thrive in the midst of them. *Remember*—prayer is not just a way for us to get things *from* God, but rather, prayer is the way for us to get *to* God. In His presence is where we find answers to every question, a resolution to every problem, and rest for our weary souls. Therefore, stop COMPLAINING and start PRAYING!

~THINK ABOUT IT~

Does what you know about God's character and His Word cause you to trust Him even during times of uncertainty and adversity in life? Have you developed a consistent daily quiet time to be with the Lord in prayer and study of His Word?

Write down on the lines below your answers to these important questions. Then write out your personal plans to strengthen your walk with the Lord in these areas.

_____
_____
_____
_____
_____
_____
_____
_____
_____
_____
_____
_____
_____
_____
_____
_____
_____
_____
_____
_____

Time With God Prayer

Father God, help your children trust your heart, even when they can't trace your hands or track your steps. Allow your joy to overflow in their hearts even during the most difficult seasons of life, knowing that you are with them always. Amen.

Meditate on Psalm 73. Write out on the lines below your personal prayer of confession, praise, and faith. Ask for STRENGTH to live holy in the midst of a crooked and perverse generation.

_____
_____
_____
_____
_____
_____
_____
_____
_____
_____
_____
_____
_____
_____
_____
_____
_____
_____

In Jesus' name, I pray, Amen.

This page intentionally left blank.

Day Four
The Joy of the Lord is Your STRENGTH

Then he said to them, Go your way, eat the fat, drink the sweet, and send portions to those for whom nothing is prepared; for this day is holy to our Lord. Do not sorrow, for the joy of the LORD is your strength (Nehemiah 8:10).

Joy—defined as delight, pleasure, bliss, ecstasy, elation, thrill, gladness, glee, rapture, wonder and happiness. Usually, when we think of "joy," we automatically think of "happiness." They both seem to go together like two peas in a pod. Does this mean these two kindred words are one and the same? Not at all. Happiness is the contentment we experience when *things happening* around us and to us (or happening to those we love and care about) are going well. However, *joy* can be experienced even in the midst of trials, tribulations and tough times of suffering.

For the believer, *joy* transcends happiness because joy is not centered in, dependent upon, or tied to your current circumstance, situation or life issues. In the book of Nehemiah, the prophet made this quite clear as he consoled the children of Israel when they began to weep after hearing the laws and judgments of God. The people wept bitterly because they failed miserably when their current lifestyle was compared to what God required of them as *His holy people*. But Nehemiah looked past the people's frailties to God's promises and possibilities—then he encouraged them.

"Then he said to them, Go your way, eat the fat, drink the sweet, and send portions to those for whom nothing is prepared; for this day is holy to our Lord. Do not sorrow, for the joy of the LORD is your strength" (Nehemiah 8:10).

Needless to say, God's "holy people" didn't feel very happy in their current situation, but they could still experience joy!

A former pastor of mine would often say to the congregation, *"You do know that God is not necessarily concerned with your happiness, don't you?"*

Well, it took some time for me to actually wrap my mind around this declaration from a man I deemed as a spiritual mentor and father in the faith. After all, why wouldn't God—my Heavenly Father and the one who loves me so much He gave his only son as a ransom for me and many—want me to be happy?

As I later pondered and prayed about the startling revelation that *God was not necessarily concerned about the happiness of the believer*, the Holy Spirit gently revealed to me a simple truth. God's ultimate concern is for our salvation and the spiritual growth and maturity of the believer in Christ Jesus, which does not always translate into a *"happy"* experience, especially during the pruning and transformation process.

Wow! This was truly an eye-opener for me, and I'm sure it may be the same for many other believers. As God prunes away the things (customs, culture, habits, hang-ups and values) of this world from the believer's life, and the things of the spirit begin to take on new meaning and priority, the spiritual transformation cycle continues, until one day, there will be a complete metamorphosis! *"For now* [in this time of imperfection] *we see in a mirror dimly* [a blurred reflection, a riddle, an enigma], *but then* [when the time of perfection comes we will see reality] *face to face. Now I know in part* [just in fragments], *but then I will know fully, just as I have been fully known* [by God]" (1 Corinthians 13:12, AMP).

So, remain encouraged and remember this as you are *being transformed daily*. In order to *live* for Christ, you must *die* to self—daily. God's pruning process can be painful, but it's necessary. The joy of the Lord is your *STRENGTH*!

"*Beloved, now we are children of God; and it has not yet been revealed what we shall be, but we know that when He is revealed, we shall be like Him, for we shall see Him as He is. And everyone who has this hope in Him purifies himself, just as He is pure*" (1 John 3:2-3).

~THINK ABOUT IT~

Read Romans 12:1-2. How does your current lifestyle compare to what God requires from *His holy people*? Although your current physical, emotional, moral and spiritual condition may not be a "happy" one, you can refresh your faith and soar to new heights as God renews your *STRENGTH* to live a victorious Christian life!

Write down on the lines below those things needing transformation in your life and specific reasons why you can rejoice in the Lord even now.

_____
_____
_____
_____
_____
_____
_____
_____
_____
_____
_____
_____
_____
_____
_____
_____
_____

Time With God Prayer

Heavenly Father, help your children humble themselves in your presence – daily. Search hearts and reveal any wicked ways that water down our witness for you. Grant the fortitude needed each day to press past our pain and problems to your promises, knowing that happiness is fleeting, but joy lasts always. Lord, give those who seek you joy and STRENGTH for the journey! In Jesus' holy name, amen.

Meditate on Isaiah 29:18-20. Write out on the lines below your personal prayer and supplication for experiencing the JOY of the Lord!

_____
_____
_____
_____
_____
_____
_____
_____
_____
_____
_____
_____
_____
_____
_____
_____
_____

In Jesus' name, I pray, Amen.

Day Five
Is Your BUT Bigger Than Your God?

Behold, I am the LORD, the God of all flesh. Is there anything too hard for Me? (Jeremiah 32:27)

One day, while talking to a young Christian woman about a certain traumatic situation that occurred in her life, I asked if she had prayed about it and asked God to deliver her from unforgiveness. I shared with her that until she was able to forgive the wrongs done and release the experience and the person responsible to God, she would remain in turmoil—physically, mentally and spiritually—and would have no peace. Her response was similar to ones I have heard many times before—and even one you or I may have given in the past.

Sobbing, she quickly and quietly responded, "Yes, I've prayed about it. BUT, you don't understand what I'm going through!"

Perhaps your response to certain situations in your life was something similar to this young woman's. Maybe you found yourself too often saying something like, "I've prayed, BUT you don't know what it's like," or "I've prayed, BUT it's too hard to let go," or "I've prayed, BUT I could never forgive him/her/myself."

Do any of these "BUT" statements sound familiar to you? Well, you are certainly not alone.

We've all more than likely been there at one time or another in our life's journey. We've prayed and prayed about a problem or situation that seemed to grow bigger and bigger with every passing day. I'm sure this is how the prophet Jeremiah felt about the children of Israel in Jerusalem and Judah. Although he prayed and prayed that they would stop worshipping idols and turn their hearts back to the true and living God, it appeared hopeless as he watched them fall deeper and deeper into sin, iniquity and shame. Their ingratitude and sinful response to the favor and blessings of God lead them into Babylonian captivity under the tyrannical rule of King Nebuchadnezzar.

As the story goes, the Babylonian army besieged Jerusalem, and Jeremiah, the prophet of the Lord, was imprisoned in the king of Judah's house. As if that were not a sad enough situation, the current physical and spiritual state of the children of Israel negated the possibility of them ever being able to return home to Jerusalem and Judah.

Things looked grim all around, to say the least. However, in the midst of such a tragic and hopeless situation, God spoke to the prophet Jeremiah a word that went against all odds. *"I will gather them out of all countries where I have driven them in My anger, in My fury, and in great wrath; I will bring them back to this place, and I will cause them to dwell safely."* (Jeremiah 32:37)

Wow—look at God! Out of chaos, God promises to bring order. In the middle of utter hopelessness, He promises to give hope and bring restoration to his people. Instead of dwelling in a foreign land in fear and danger, God promises safety in their own land. When it comes right down to it, there is nothing in this life (or the life beyond) that is bigger than our God! So, I ask again, *"Is your BUT bigger than your God?"*

"Behold, I am the LORD, the God of all flesh. Is there anything too hard for Me?" (Jeremiah 32:27)

~THINK ABOUT IT~

What are you facing in your life today that may have caused you to focus on the size of the "BUT" in your situation or circumstance rather than focusing on the immeasurable size of your God? I encourage you to look beyond what you can see with the natural eye, and in the spirit, see the unseen, invisible, intangible! It's there that you will find God's hand in your circumstance.

Write down on the lines below those things from your past and present that you may have perceived impossible. Then release them to God in believing prayer.

_____
_____
_____
_____
_____
_____
_____
_____
_____
_____
_____
_____
_____
_____
_____
_____
_____
_____

Time With God Prayer

Father God, thank you for being bigger than our BUT's! Help us to always look past the unseen and trust in your ability to do the impossible – no matter how impossible it may seem. Amen.

Meditate on Philippians 4:13. Write out on the lines below your personal prayer of release and acceptance of God to do the impossible in your life.

_____
_____
_____
_____
_____
_____
_____
_____
_____
_____
_____
_____
_____
_____
_____
_____
_____
_____
_____
_____

In Jesus' name, I pray, Amen.

This page intentionally left blank.

Day Six
Somebody Bigger

I will say of the LORD, "He is my refuge and my fortress; My God, in Him I will trust. Surely He shall deliver you from the snare of the fowler and from the perilous pestilence. He shall cover you with His feathers, and under His wings you shall take refuge; His truth shall be your shield and buckler. You shall not be afraid of the terror by night, nor of the arrow that flies by day, Nor of the pestilence that walks in darkness, Nor of the destruction that lay waste at noonday (Psalm 91:2-6).

When you think of God's omnipotence and sovereignty, what do you think about? To whom can you compare Him? Singer/songwriter, VaShawn Mitchell, declared that he "searched all over" and "couldn't find anyone" to compare to the Lord. ("Nobody Greater," 2011)

Oftentimes, due to life's obnoxious obstacles and relentless roadblocks, I found myself seeking the sovereign savior's guidance and direction. Dreams delayed and goals deferred due to unforeseen hurdles, turns, and detours in life led me to turn back the pages of my memory and reflect upon God's sovereign and omnipotent hand in the middle of my life circumstances.

During those times, I often remember the lyrics to an old gospel song entitled "Somebody Bigger Than You and I." (Johnny Lange, Hy Heath and Sonny Burke, 1951.)

I encourage you to take a few minutes to listen to both of these songs on YouTube or Amazon Music. Many artists recorded both songs, so take your pick of which version you like best.

When facing a multitude of setbacks, upsets and uncertainties in life, it's very easy to focus on our problems instead of on our "problem-solver." The song "Somebody Bigger Than You and I" is an epic reminder of God's supreme creativity, eternal faithfulness, absolute power, and boundless love—timeless in its message.

In Psalm 91, the Psalmist (possibly Moses) was also aware of this ecclesiastical nature, character and power of God as he described Him as "covering us with His feathers to protect us in times of trouble," just like a bird protects her babies in order to shield them from any hurt, harm or danger (vs. 2-4). The Psalmist goes on to say that because we are under God's personal protection—a place of safety, refuge and a tower of strength—we don't have to worry about hidden dangers (snares), deadly diseases (pestilence), or any other type of destruction because God is bigger than anything that can come against us!

In Jeremiah 32:27, God says, *"Behold, I am Jehovah, the God of all flesh: is there anything too hard for me?"*

Of course, this is a rhetorical question, but many times we act as if it is not. We often respond, react and combat life situations and circumstances in a manner that implies the contrary as we agonize about the past, present and future losses, dangers and possible adverse outcomes.

God wants us to be secure in His sovereign power and protection, but we must totally surrender to Him. A totally surrendered life means trusting God completely with your past, present and future. Proverbs 3:5-6 says, *"Trust in the Lord with all your heart, and lean not to your own understanding. In all your ways acknowledge Him, and he shall direct your path."* As Christ-followers, Jesus is our ultimate example, especially when it comes to living a surrendered lifestyle. Jesus totally surrendered to God's ultimate plan for the salvation of man.

He prayed, "Nevertheless, not my will Lord, but your will be done."

Genuine surrender of the will says, "If I have to go through this problem, pain, sickness, or circumstance in order to fulfill the perfect will of God, then... Nevertheless, Lord, not my will, but your will be done."

This is a level of spiritual maturity that many believers may never achieve, but that does not mean we should not keep on striving to achieve it—step-by-step, trial-by-trial— *"Surrender yourself to the Lord, and wait patiently for Him"* (Psalm 37:7a, GW).

A life totally surrendered to God trusts and depends upon Him to work things out instead of putting faith in personal resources, worldly connections, and tangible possessions. Of course, this does not mean that believers should not utilize every opportunity and resource God provides. However, it does mean that a life surrendered to God does not try to manipulate people and force personal agendas to control situations and circumstances. A life surrendered to God does not need to use foul language and physical force to defend or feel better about oneself. A surrendered life does not put trust in the "almighty dollar," but rather such a life places trust in "God-Almighty." A totally surrendered life is one lived like there is *Somebody Bigger than You and I*.

~THINK ABOUT IT~

A surrendered life is not "self-serving," but rather "God-pleasing." In order to truly live a surrendered life for the glory of the Lord, what area(s) of your life do you need to surrender to God today? Saying, "Not my will, Lord, but your will be done," write your "list of surrender" on the lines below.

_____
_____
_____
_____
_____
_____
_____
_____
_____
_____
_____
_____
_____
_____
_____
_____
_____
_____
_____
_____
_____
_____

Time With God Prayer

Father God, You are my refuge and STRENGTH. All of my help and hope are in you alone. I freely surrender all to your will and to your way. In Jesus' name, I pray. Amen

Meditate on Psalm 91. Write out on the lines below your personal prayer of surrender and faith.

_____
_____
_____
_____
_____
_____
_____
_____
_____
_____
_____
_____
_____
_____
_____
_____
_____
_____
_____
_____

In Jesus' name, I pray, Amen.

This page intentionally left blank.

Day Seven
God is Our Refuge and STRENGTH

God is our refuge and our strength, a very present help in trouble. Therefore we will not fear, even though the earth be removed, and though the mountains be carried into the midst of the sea; though its waters roar and be troubled, though the mountains shake with its swelling. Selah. There is a river whose streams shall make glad the city of God, the holy place of the tabernacle of the Most High (Psalm 46:1-4).

Perhaps you've found yourself in trouble. Whether self-inflicted or Satan's snares—trouble is *trouble* all the same. Trouble can take on many forms—worry about a wayward child, anxiety over marital issues, distress over a declining stock market, or suffering from deteriorating health. T*rouble* can cause your *journey* to be less gratifying, to say the least.

Psalm 46 was believed to be written during the Babylonian exile of the Israelites during a time of darkness, filled with woe and despair and the enemy seemingly triumphant over God's people. It was at their lowest and most troublesome time that the Psalmist penned the words of the 46th Psalm to bring the people hope and encouragement in the face of clear and present danger.

As a believer, take comfort in knowing this—you never have to face *trouble* all alone. As you travel life's journey and times become difficult at best, know that you can turn to God to find *inner strength* when needed—strength to stand steadfast through hard times and walk unwaveringly through the raging storms of life.

Regardless of what you may be facing, or what may be facing you, be encouraged—God is near! Yes, know that God is present in the midst of the madness, problems and pain. So, beloved, encourage yourself with these words, just as the Psalmist encouraged the children of Israel when he proclaimed, *"God is our refuge and our strength, a very present help in trouble"* (Psalm 46:1).

Time and time again, the Bible reminds us of God's great power and capability of restoring and renewing our strength. The prophet appeals to the weak and the weary believer in Isaiah 40:29-31. He reminds us of God's great power and might and His ability to turn around any seemingly hopeless situation. *However*, God's promise to give power to the weak, increase and renew the strength (*exchange your strength for His*) of those who are faltering and failing comes with a condition—WAIT. The challenge now becomes this—*how good are you at waiting on the Lord?*

Consider the story of Joshua and Caleb as they (and the others selected) went to scout out the "promised land" prior to the children of Israel going up to lay claim on it. Upon returning to camp, the report of the majority to the leaders of their visual assessment of the land of Canaan was bleak. Nevertheless, Caleb resolved to trust God's promise—no matter what he had seen. *"Then Caleb quieted the people before Moses, and said, "Let us go up at once and take possession, for we are well able to overcome it"* (Numbers 13:30). Caleb had the courage and strength to boldly go up and possess a land filled with giants because his *focus* was in the right place—on the magnitude of his God, not the size of the giants! Do you have giants to conquer in your life? *Then where is your focus today?*

The message to the children of Israel then, and even to God's children today, is this—when *troubles* trouble you, remember God, and only GOD, is your safe house, hiding place, and the source of your STRENGTH. *Stay focused, wait in faith and watch your fears fade!*

~*THINK ABOUT IT*~

When the storms of life are raging, make sure Jesus is the Captain of your soul. It's better to ride the waves of life with God's saving grace, love and mercy as your compass instead of being stuck in the sands of sin on the shore. Jesus alone can guide you safely to port and say, "fear not—all is well."

Think about rocky times in your life. Write down on the lines below how you feel the Lord's hand of mercy, grace and love helped you endure and guided you safely through those times of trouble.

_____
_____
_____
_____
_____
_____
_____
_____
_____
_____
_____
_____
_____
_____
_____
_____
_____
_____
_____
_____

Time With God Prayer

Father God, thank you for being our hope when hopeless, our help when helpless, and our strength when we feel defeated by the enemy and cruelty of this world. Hide us in the safety of your loving arms, protect us from seen and unseen dangers, and renew our strength so that we might endure in tumultuous times like these. Thank you for being our ever-present help in times of trouble. Help us to praise you at all times, knowing without a shadow of a doubt that our help and STRENGTH is in you, oh Lord! Amen.

Meditate on Psalm 117. Write out on the lines below your personal prayer of praise, acknowledging God as your refuge and STRENGTH in times of trouble.

_____
_____
_____
_____
_____
_____
_____
_____
_____
_____
_____
_____
_____
_____

In Jesus' name, I pray, Amen.

This page intentionally left blank.

Day Eight
Such as I Have

Then Peter said, "Silver and gold have I none; but such as I have, give I thee: In the name of Jesus Christ of Nazareth rise up and walk (Acts 3:6, KJV).

It's amazing how often we put so much value in temporal things that have no eternal value. Most of our lives are spent collecting perishable mementos that we will leave behind when we pass from this mortal realm. We spend countless hours and miss precious moments with those we love, all in an exasperating effort to climb the corporate ladder. We keep our nose to the grind and our head down without even seeing God's beauty all around as we continue to push our way up to the top. Then one day, you arrive! You now have that dream house, the kids are grown and gone, the bank accounts are bulging, and you can now finally retire and really begin to enjoy life.

This is exactly what the rich farmer thought after his fertile farmland consistently produced bumper crops year after year. In fact, his barns bulged at the seams with an overflow of produce to the point that he had no more space. After thinking long and hard about his surplus situation and limited space problem, he decided to tear down his barns and build bigger barns to store his overflow of food. After he resolved that dilemma, it was time to plan his retirement and party hearty! (Luke 12:16-21).

This seemed like a great plan to the rich man, and perhaps

to many of us, but God called him a *"fool."* Why? Surely not because he was wise and prosperous in the agricultural arena and made perpetual plans for his future. Of course not. It was because God looked upon his heart and found no plans for his eternal life (Luke 12:20-21).

Real life and "living" is not equivalent to monetary value or the abundance of material things possessed while here on planet earth. Spending all of your time getting fat with materialistic wealth and riches while allowing your soul to go undernourished and your spiritual bank account to run dry will result in a severe case of spiritual malnutrition and a fatal eternal outcome. This is certainly not wise, especially for the believer.

The lesson Jesus taught in the parable of *"The Rich Fool"* is also what the Apostle Peter demonstrated when he encountered the lame beggar at *"The Gate Beautiful."* This man, lame from birth, had been carried to the temple every day, but not to pray. Little did he know that today would be a good day for him. Not because he would receive loads of loot from those passing by, but because he would receive bountiful blessings through a man that was willing to be used for God's kingdom-building business—in spite of not having earthly treasures.

"Then Peter said, silver and gold have I none; but such as I have, give I thee: In the name of Jesus Christ of Nazareth rise up and walk." (Acts 3:6, KJV).

The rich farmer never once thought about sharing what he had with the underprivileged, poor and starving. And although Peter didn't have any money to share with the lame beggar, what he did have, he was more than willing to share—something money could not buy. The results were miraculous! A man that had gone to the temple every day, but never entered to pray, was now entering the temple with

Peter and John for the first time, walking, leaping, and praising God! Not only did these two men of God help bring about an immediate physical restoration for the lame man, they also initiated an eternal impact for him. And the added bonus? Those who witnessed the miracle would never be the same!

~THINK ABOUT IT~

MORAL: Be careful of the things you desire to possess, because one day, they just might possess you! Are you willing to say "such as I have" to someone in need of seeing the Jesus in you today?

Think about how your quest for material things may have hindered your desire to seek the spiritual. Write down on the lines below your spirit-inspired thoughts and actions to take.

_____
_____
_____
_____
_____
_____
_____
_____
_____
_____
_____
_____
_____
_____
_____
_____
_____
_____
_____
_____
_____
_____
_____

Time With God Prayer

Father God, give us a heart for the lost, sick and hurting. Let us not be entangled in the web of materialism, but rather give us a desire to seek hard after things of the spirit. Lord, help your children to realize that you alone are more than enough! In Jesus' name, I pray, Amen.

Meditate on Psalm 115. Write out on the lines below your personal prayer of praise and thanksgiving for God's trustworthiness and faithfulness.

_____
_____
_____
_____
_____
_____
_____
_____
_____
_____
_____
_____
_____
_____
_____
_____
_____
_____

In Jesus' name, I pray, Amen.

Day Nine
Lord, STRENGTHEN My Hands

For they all were trying to make us afraid, saying, "Their hands will be weakened in the work, and it will not be done." Now therefore, O God, strengthen my hands (Nehemiah 6:9).

The Old-Testament Prophet, Nehemiah, was on assignment from God. He was commissioned by God to spearhead the rebuilding of the city walls of Jerusalem. But as it would be, the enemy made every attempt to sabotage the work—even to the extent of plotting to kill Nehemiah.

When the prophet would not succumb to the enemy's tricks and tactics to lure him down from work on the wall, they sent a false prophet with a message intended to instill fear into the heart of Nehemiah and lead him into sin against God (Nehemiah 6:1-8).

More times than not, when troubles, trials and tribulations land at our front door, we immediately begin to search for another *"way out."* However, perhaps your way of escape is simply through *endurance*—trusting God to see you *through* that difficult situation or circumstance. The reality is this—God never promised that the Christian life would be easy. But, God did promise He would never leave or forsake you—even though you may walk through the valley and the shadow of death (Psalm 23). God promises to be right there with you, leading, guiding, holding and STRENGTHENING you every step of the way!

Nehemiah recognized the enemy's deception. What they

proposed he do in order to flee imminent danger contradicted the word he received directly from God (Nehemiah 6:10-13). Being Christian means to be chosen for a kingdom purpose — just like Nehemiah. Many times the enemy will attempt any and all forms of trickery, traps and schemes in order to derail you from that purpose and make you too afraid to finish the work you've been called to do. Nehemiah went through numerous attempts of the enemy to sabotage his work. Various forms of fear tactics were used to distract him, people plotted to take his life, and he even withstood a fierce attempt of the enemy to lead him into sin.

During your moments of weakness, when others (and perhaps even you) may feel that you can't go on, be encouraged. Just like Nehemiah, you can and will finish what God called and equipped you to accomplish.

Just remember the words of the Prophet Nehemiah. *"Now therefore, O God, strengthen my hands."* Be assured that God will give you the *strength* needed to complete the work and the journey.

"So the wall was finished on the twenty-fifth day of Elul, in fifty-two days" (Nehemiah 6:15).

~THINK ABOUT IT~

Have you been wondering how you're going to get beyond what you've been going through? Just know that some painful things you may go through are not really all about you. They are simply labor pains for the ministry that's about to be birth through you! The biggest fish are caught in the deepest waters. Regardless of what it may look like, launch out into the deep waters of FAITH where the biggest and best blessings await you.

Write on the lines below any spirit-inspired thoughts or God-given revelations regarding situations you may currently be experiencing and areas of faith that need to be released in your life. *(Note: Ask God to give you new insight, understanding and clarity concerning those areas that may have previously caused you worry, confusion, doubt, fear or hesitation.)*

_____
_____
_____
_____
_____
_____
_____
_____
_____
_____
_____
_____
_____
_____

Time With God Prayer

Father God, help your children not to be dismayed when encountering the enemy's attack, but instead to pray for your STRENGTH to endure. Open the spiritual eyes of your children so that in difficult times, they see you above all they may go through, realizing that you endured the nails so they might now prevail. In Jesus' strong and mighty name I pray, Amen.

Meditate on Jeremiah 33:3. Write out on the lines below your personal prayer for strength and endurance to get through a specific situation in your life.

_____
_____
_____
_____
_____
_____
_____
_____
_____
_____
_____
_____
_____
_____
_____
_____
_____

In Jesus' name, I pray, Amen.

Day Ten
Speak No Evil

Don't use foul or abusive language. Let everything you say be good and helpful, so that your words will be an encouragement to those who hear them (Ephesians 4:29, NLT).

Some little things have enormous power. For instance, consider ants. They are small, yet they can move things three times their size. A small rudder can propel a huge boat across deep waters. Pea-sized hail can cause astronomical damage to houses, cars and property. A cry of distress from a newborn baby can bring an entire household to a screeching halt. And the list can go on and on when you begin to ponder the power of little things.

There is no doubt that little things can make a big impact on our lives. When you consider the "tongue" in comparison to other parts of the human anatomy, it may not seem as significant. But it is a powerful thing!

This small part of the human body can be used for good or evil, to bring joy or pain, to build up or tear down. The mouth can be used as a conduit for uplifting and encouraging, or it can be dastardly and devastating to others, based upon the words that come forth from it.

"If anyone does not stumble in word, he is a perfect man, able also to bridle the whole body" (James 3:2b).

Take a moment to self-reflect on your verbal history. How have you used your mouth lately? Perhaps in prayer, encouragement, motivation, and blessings—even to praise your Savior and Lord. Maybe you have used your words as a "secret weapon" when you've gotten into conflict or arguments, or perhaps to strike back at someone you feel has wronged you—even to tear down and curse those who were created in the likeness of God. Praises and curses coming forth from the same mouth—the Apostle James speaks against these things.

"Out of the same mouth proceed blessing and cursing. My brethren, these things ought not to be so" (James 3:10).

According to the Bible, the old adage *"sticks and stones may break my bones, but words will never harm me"* is the farthest thing from the truth. Little words seem small in size, but they can pack a big punch!

Words can, and do, destroy relationships and lives. Therefore, God wants His children to think about the power of the spoken word as it relates to encouraging and building up one another.

"Don't use foul or abusive language. Let everything you say be good and helpful, so that your words will be an encouragement to those who hear them" (Ephesians 4:29, NLT).

In other words, *Speak No Evil!*

~THINK ABOUT IT~

Do you sometimes use your "words" in an ungodly way? Do you use the "power of the spoken word" to build people up or to tear them down? What do you need to change about the way you use the power of the tongue? As you ponder these questions, pray and ask God to help you use your words as a "fresh-water spring," bringing life to all who hear!

Write on the lines below any spirit-inspired thoughts that will help you "speak life" into others and yourself.

_____
_____
_____
_____
_____
_____
_____
_____
_____
_____
_____
_____
_____
_____
_____
_____
_____
_____
_____
_____

Time With God Prayer

Father God, help your children speak life into every dead situation! Help our words bring blessings and not curses to those you have created in your image and become fresh water to thirsty souls who hear them. In Jesus' name, I pray. Amen.

Meditate on Psalm 34:13-14. Write out on the lines below your personal prayer to keep your mouth from speaking evil and deceit and to be used as a fresh-water spring of blessings.

_____
_____
_____
_____
_____
_____
_____
_____
_____
_____
_____
_____
_____
_____
_____
_____
_____
_____

In Jesus' name, I pray, Amen.

This page intentionally left blank.

Day Eleven
What's in a Name?

And He said, "Your name shall no longer be called Jacob, but Israel; for you have struggled with God and with men, and have prevailed." (Genesis 32:28)

"What's in a name? That which we call a rose by any other name would smell as sweet." ~ Shakespeare

Most people are very familiar with this famous quote taken from the popular play *Romeo and Juliet* by William Shakespeare. This play is the epitome of Shakespeare's poetic genius when it comes to portraying a love to die for.

Although I may agree with the fact that the "*name*" of a rose does not change the "*smell*" of it, the Bible takes a very different stance on the importance of "*a name*" when it comes to His creations.

After God created the beast of the field and the birds of the air, He commissioned Adam with the very special task of naming them all. "*Out of the ground, the LORD God formed every beast of the field and every bird of the air and brought them to Adam to see what he would call them. And whatever Adam called each living creature – that was its name. So Adam gave names to all cattle, to the birds of the air, and to every beast of the field*" (Genesis 2:19-20).

But, God didn't stop with the creation of the beasts and the birds. He also created a helper for Adam, and Adam named her as well. "*And the LORD God caused a deep sleep to fall on Adam, and he slept; and He took one of his ribs, and closed up the flesh in its place. Then the rib which the LORD God had taken from man He made into a woman, and He brought her to the man. And Adam said: "This is now bone of my bones and flesh of my flesh; she shall be called Woman, because she was taken out of Man"* (Genesis 2:21-23).

Subsequently, the importance of "a name" was established with mankind. In the Hebrew culture, names were very important because they exemplified the essence of who you were—like the name Jacob, which means deceiver or trickster. But after an all-night wrestling match with God on the night before he was to reunite with his estranged brother, Esau, God changed Jacob's name to *Israel*, which means *"struggle or wrestle with God and prevail."*

Yes, there was something more to Jacob than what he demonstrated in the past. God saw "Israel," an overcomer! Israel, not Jacob, was someone who would prevail because of his persistence to be right with God and man. *"And He said, 'Your name shall no longer be called Jacob, but Israel; for you have struggled with God and with men, and have prevailed'"* (Genesis 32:1-28).

Recently, I drove in a neighborhood and noticed the names of the streets were named after animals, mostly birds, like "Bald Eagle Way" and "Sky Hawks Lane." But, as I looked around the neighborhood, I didn't see any evidence of these majestic birds still in existence today. Then it dawned on me. Those streets may have been named based on what *"use to be"* normal sights in the area decades ago. In other words, the streets were named after what the area *"used to look like,"* not the present reality.

The importance of a name should still stand true today. How many times has someone from your past come back into your life, and without thought, they automatically called you by the "nickname" they used to call you by back in the day? That nickname may have represented who you were back then, but it may no longer adequately or justly describe who you are today.

There is a saying that goes like this—"*It's not what someone calls you, but what you answer to that matters.*" So I ask you—are you still answering to names that explicitly describe who you "*used to be,*" but not who you are now since Jesus' hand of salvation touched you, and *He changed your name?*

~THINK ABOUT IT~

Yes, "a name" can and does make a difference. By nature, Peter was very impetuous. He acted impulsively, responded out of anger, and spoke rashly. However, Jesus saw something in Peter that he had not yet lived up to as a Disciple but would eventually become. So Jesus changed Simon's name to Peter, translated Cephas in Hebrew, which means "The Rock" (John 1:42). It took a while before impetuous Peter became "The Rock," but Jesus looked past his present state and called him what he would become. What's inside of you waiting to break free? Can you hear Jesus calling you by your new name? Write on the lines below what you hear the Spirit of the Lord calling you today.

_____
_____
_____
_____
_____
_____
_____
_____
_____
_____
_____
_____
_____
_____
_____
_____

Time With God Prayer

Father God, help your children think of themselves as you think of them – to see themselves as you see them and to speak of themselves as you have already spoken into them, allowing the Holy Spirit to manifest in and through them all you have ordained. It's in Jesus' matchless name I pray and give you all the glory! Amen.

Meditate on Matthew 16:18-20. Write out on the lines below your personal prayer to believe and become all God desires.

_____
_____
_____
_____
_____
_____
_____
_____
_____
_____
_____
_____
_____
_____
_____
_____
_____
_____

In Jesus' name, I pray, Amen.

This page intentionally left blank.

Day Twelve
Ministry Matters

Let nothing be done through selfish ambition or conceit, but in lowliness of mind let each esteem others better than himself. Let each of you look out not only for his own interests, but also for the interests of others (Philippians 2:3-4).

There are multitudes of what we call "mega-churches" today. Many believers seek out this type of church, sometimes for the wrong reasons. Although they know it's "right" to be in a church (membership), they don't really want to get too involved. Often, these individuals seek out a church with a congregation large enough that they will not be noticed as they quietly move in and out on Sunday mornings.

On the other hand, you have believers who shy away from large church congregations, attempting to avoid "the crowds." Even when their church congregation begins to grow too much, they move on to another "smaller church," saying, *"A small church feels more like family, and the Pastor knows everybody's name."*

Both these types of reasoning are extremes, and the believer should beware not to fall prey to either scenario. Attempting to get lost in the masses or settling for a church that is stagnated in growth—neither is pleasing to God. After all, anything that does not grow is dead!

God created "the church" for many reasons, but His intent was never for the church to remain small and secluded. *"And the Lord added to the church daily those who were being saved"* (Acts 2:47).

As more and more souls are added, your "church family" may begin to grow by leaps and bounds. This is a wonderful thing! But, it may also be a little scary for some as they see their cozy little church family beginning to bulge at the seams. Your church may experience changes, such as the number of worship services on Sunday morning, increasing to accommodate the expanding congregation. People pass by you, entering the sanctuary, that you don't even know—especially if you happen to attend a different worship service than usual. Not to mention that uneasy feeling of being lost in the masses with the growing fear that your pastor is becoming "untouchable."

However, as this congregation transformation happens, it is the responsibility of each church member to make sure you stay connected—not only connected to Christ but connected to other believers within the church. The "church house" is not only a place where the people of God gather to learn and grow in Christ, it is also a place for believers to come together as a community to support, encourage, love and fellowship together. In order not to get lost in the crowd of people—feeling like you are alone and don't matter—get involved in small groups and volunteer in a ministry.

The church is not only a place for others within and outside of the community to come and receive help, but it is also a place where the body of believers can receive and give help, encouragement, love and support to others.

As you get involved in serving others through ministry, you also forge, foster and build relationships with others in your church family and community.

"The believers shared a common purpose, and every day they spent much of their time together in the Temple area. They also ate together in their homes. They were happy to share their food and ate

with joyful hearts. The believers praised God and were respected by all the people. More and more people were being saved every day, and the Lord was adding them to their group" (Acts 2:46-47, ERV).

These relationships are the stepping stones to birth true ministry—inside and outside the church house walls. The Bible says we should pity the one who falls and has no one to help them up (Ecclesiastes 4:10). Being involved in ministry also provides a support group for the believer. No matter how large your congregation grows, you will always have a group of people within the church body who will be there for you when life situations happen, and you need the love, support, encouragement and prayers of your church family.

Therefore, being a member of the church body is not a "spectator sport." You will never experience the fellowship, love, sharing and caring the church is designed by God to experience standing on the outside looking in. You have to get involved! You are saved-to-serve.

"Let nothing be done through selfish ambition or conceit, but in lowliness of mind let each esteem others better than himself. Let each of you look out not only for his own interests, but also for the interests of others" (Philippians 2:3-4).

God wants every church member to become more than just a spectator or a consumer. No more "dead sea" saints (believers only taking in), but rather becoming transformed into "red sea" saints—bringing hope and help to those crossing over into a new life! God wants you to *"grow"* so that you will "know" and can *"go"* for Him. Don't delay. Get started today. *Ministry Matters!*

~THINK ABOUT IT~

Have you been a part of the church body for a while but have never really gotten involved? Is the extent of your fellowship with the body of believers little more than a simple "good morning" or "hello" on Sunday mornings? Well, it's time for you to get off the sideline and get connected! Start by getting a list of ministries currently available at your church and pray for God's guidance in the area of ministry in which He would have you serve. Write down on the lines below the names of those ministries and how you feel the Holy Spirit is leading you to serve in the body of Christ.

_____
_____
_____
_____
_____
_____
_____
_____
_____
_____
_____
_____
_____
_____
_____
_____

Time With God Prayer

Father God, help your children truly "be the church," not simply satisfied with going to church. Reveal your will, Father, to those seeking direction in the area of service and ministry. It's in Jesus' name I pray, Amen.

Meditate on Philippians 2:4. Write out on the lines below your personal prayer to be used by God in his service to others.

_____
_____
_____
_____
_____
_____
_____
_____
_____
_____
_____
_____
_____
_____
_____
_____
_____
_____
_____

In Jesus' name, I pray, Amen.

Day Thirteen
Seeking God First

But seek first the kingdom of God and His righteousness, and all these things shall be added to you (Matthew 6:33).

Shortly after we were married, my husband and I committed to starting out every New Year with a period of prayer and fasting—seeking God's will and plan for our family, ministry, and lives as we moved into another year together. We knew that if we truly wanted to honor God with our marriage, and if we sincerely wanted to be used by God in a supernatural way to minister to others and make a difference in the lives of those we encounter, then we must seek God's guidance and direction first.

This particular year was no different as we committed together to seek God first as we launched out into new beginnings. Usually, as we fast and pray together, God speaks into us the direction He desires us to take specifically regarding ministry.

However, this time, God gently whispered to me, *"Be ready."* This two-word message was planted like a seed deep down within my soul. As we continued to seek God's face through prayer and fasting, this Rhema word continued to resound in my ears, mind and heart. *"Be ready."* God then further revealed to me the reason why. We wouldn't have time to "get ready." We needed to already *"be ready."*

I thought, okay Lord, but *"be ready"* for what?

Whatever the Lord ordained or allowed.

As I reflect back on that year, and the years since then, I stand in awe of God's boundless strength, matchless mercy, and never-ending goodness in our lives. As I reminisce on all of the mountain-top highs, valley lows, melancholy moments, and even days of ecstatic delight, I see God's sovereign love, mercy and grace in them all. From going through a major life-threatening illness, disease and death with dearly beloved ones in our family to celebrating milestones in our ministry, lives and the lives of those we love dearly. But, the constant through it all was, and will remain, God's faithfulness!

The balancing of marriage, family, ministry and work has not been easy, but it has been a blessing. As my husband and I surrendered in humble obedience to God — step-by-step and day-by-day — He faithfully provided the *STRENGTH* needed for the journey. The message of *"be ready"* overflowed into our family, ministry, church and work environments. It became the motto and launching pad for a whole new season of service — *be ready was for real*!

Our personal testimony is this — seeking God first in life has opened up windows of blessings for a healthy, happy marriage; effective ministry; loving and supportive family; life-long friendships; and a wonderful church family, just to name a few. In addition, God allowed us to accomplish major goals each year as a manifestation of His previous promises. We serve a BIG GOD, so why not expect BIG things to happen as you seek Him first!

~THINK ABOUT IT~

What is it that you desire of the Lord? Try seeking Him and his righteousness first and see what windows of opportunity and blessings will be opened unto you. Seek, submit, trust and obey—God will always make a way! The joy will be in the journey when you seek God first.

Write down on the lines below the things you desire of the Lord. Then write out your commitment to seeking Him first in your life.

_____
_____
_____
_____
_____
_____
_____
_____
_____
_____
_____
_____
_____
_____
_____
_____
_____
_____
_____
_____

Time With God Prayer

Father God, we stand on tip-toes of anticipation, expecting great things from our great God! Our hearts desire to live a life that will bring you glory and honor. Holy Spirit, have your way in us – transform us day-by-day into children who are totally pleasing to the Father in every way. We love you, Lord, so we completely surrender ourselves to you – mind, body and soul. It's in the sovereign, transforming name of Jesus Christ we pray. Amen.

Meditate on Matthew 6:25-33. Write out on the lines below your personal prayer of surrender. Acknowledge your personal desires to the Lord.

_____
_____
_____
_____
_____
_____
_____
_____
_____
_____
_____
_____
_____
_____
_____

In Jesus' name, I pray, Amen.

Day Fourteen
Seasons of Sorrows

Why are you cast down, O my soul? And why are you disquieted within me? Hope in God, for I shall yet praise Him for the help of His countenance (Psalm 42:5).

Hurricanes, wildfires, mass shootings, nuclear weapons, failed marriages, waning health, prodigal children, friends turned foe—and the list goes on and on. Satan is not our friend, and trouble seems to lurk around every corner, waiting to pounce on the believer unexpectedly.

During this life, we all experience ups and downs, times of joy and pain, and even seasons of sorrow. It's during these trying times that believers must be intentional in our faith concerning God's provision, guidance, protection, direction and deliverance. Just like the writer of the 42nd Psalm, we must yearn for God's presence even in the midst of sorrow. *"As the deer pants [longingly] for the water brooks, so my soul pants [longingly] for You, O God"* (Psalm 42:1, AMP).

Although in a depressed state due to impending danger and ridicule of his enemies, the Psalmist found himself thirsting for the living God—even in the midst of troubled times. But, how does one focus on faith and not fear, especially when the troublesome situation is overwhelmingly consuming every aspect of your being?

"My tears have been my food day and night, while they continually say unto me, 'Where is your God?'" (Psalm 42:3, ASV).

Well, let's take a lesson from the Psalmist as he shared a time in his life when he too experienced trouble to the extent that his very soul was in great despair. He felt as if the weight of it all was too much to bear.

"I will say to God my rock, "Why have you forgotten me? Why do I go mourning because of the oppression of the enemy?"" (Psalm 42:9).

Then something miraculous happened! He began to drift down memory lane, recalling a time when he was so full of joy and enthusiasm. He remembered a time when he used to lead the people to the house of God for praise and worship, like a choirmaster leading singers. All of a sudden, as he reflected upon these joyous times in the presence of the Lord, a paradigm shift in his outlook took place. This caused him to look inward [soul] and upward [God] instead of outward at his situation.

"Why are you in despair, O my soul? Why have you become restless and disquieted within me? Hope in God and wait expectantly for Him, for I shall yet praise Him, The help of my countenance and my God" (Psalm 42:11, AMP).

The Psalmist realized (and so should we) that even though he might have been distressed, he was not destroyed! Even in the middle of madness, he could still feel the power of God's presence as he longed for His love and peace to once again fill his heart, mind and soul.

Therefore, child of God, no matter what season of sorrow you might be in at the moment, refuse to allow it to hold you captive. Remember, the good thing about "seasons" is they never remain the same — they always change!

~THINK ABOUT IT~

Are you tired of carrying around the things that have held you captive for much too long? It's time to break loose and walk into your new season! When God is ready, He will open every door of impossibility. This is the appointed time. Keep the faith, listen to God's voice, and *be READY* to move in response. Your faith will unlock the impossible and set your potential free!

Think about those things holding you back or causing you distress in this season of your life and write them on the lines below.

_____
_____
_____
_____
_____
_____
_____
_____
_____
_____
_____
_____
_____
_____
_____
_____
_____

Time With God Prayer

Father God, help us truly believe that nothing is too hard for you – the omniscient, omnipresent, and omnipotent one! Give us a longing for more of you even in the midst of our pain, trusting you to do the impossible, in Jesus' name! Amen.

Meditate on Psalm 42 and Genesis 18:14. If you are in a stressful or distressing situation right now, begin to praise God in spite of your pain. And remember – if He did it before, He can do it again! Journal your personal prayer on the lines below.

_____
_____
_____
_____
_____
_____
_____
_____
_____
_____
_____
_____
_____
_____
_____
_____
_____
_____
_____

In Jesus' name, I pray, Amen.

Day Fifteen
He Will Do It!

Now may the God of peace Himself sanctify you completely; and may your whole spirit, soul, and body be preserved blameless at the coming of our Lord Jesus Christ. He who calls you is faithful, who also will do it (1Thessalonians 5:23-24).

As a believer, you have a new identity in Christ Jesus. You are being transformed day-by-day into the likeness and newness of Christ. You now have a new walk, a new talk, and a new look—a total makeover is taking place, and you are being changed!

Hold up—wait a minute! This "change" doesn't seem to come easy. As you seek to shed old habits and hang-ups for a new you in Christ, it becomes painfully clear that your newly remodeled home (mind, body, soul and spirit) has a "double-occupancy," and a war is going on in the house.

Your old nature is warring against your new nature! You are in a "tug-of-war" with SIN from within!

"So, I find it to be a law that when I want to do right, evil lies close at hand. For I delight in the law of God, in my inner being, but I see in my members another law waging war against the law of my mind and making me captive to the law of sin that dwells in my members" (Romans 7:21-23, ESV).

Every day, sin tries to win this spiritual tug-of-war—a war that every Christian was drafted into as a result of Adam and Eve taking a bite out of the big apple. After all, the pruning process is very painful, but it's necessary to become like Christ. The Apostle Paul recognized this raging war going on in his inward man, and he cried out, asking the same question many believers have asked as we tug back and forth with sin. *"Oh wretched man that I am, who shall deliver me from this body of death?"* (Romans 7:24, KJV).

Sin's provocation is rooted in the hatred of God. Satan desires to kill God, but can't, so he targets the next best thing—those whom God loves. Satan's mission is to kill, steal and destroy the saints. He wants to kill and destroy the believer in order to hurt God. Therefore, the spiritual tug-of-war within the believer continues as the enemy tries time and time again to win spiritual battles and render the believer ineffective in their witness and walk with Christ, just as he did in the story of Job.

"And the LORD said to Satan, 'Have you considered my servant Job, that there is none like him on the earth, a blameless and upright man, who fears God and turns away from evil? He still holds fast his integrity, although you incited me against him to destroy him without reason.' Then Satan answered the LORD and said, 'Skin for skin! All that a man has he will give for his life. But stretch out your hand and touch his bone and his flesh, and he will curse you to your face'" (Job 2:3-5, ESV).

But don't be dismayed. The battle is not over—victory is ultimately yours! Paul realized this same fact about his spiritual tug-of-war as he exploded in praise. *"I thank God—through Jesus Christ our Lord"* (Romans 7:25).

Just like in the game of tug-of-war, you always want your strongest team member as the "anchor" in order to have the advantage and greatest chance of winning. Guess what? Jesus Christ is your anchorman—you WIN! *"He who calls you is faithful, who also will do it"* (1Thessalonians 5:24).

~THINK ABOUT IT~

What then? Shall we keep on sinning so that God can show us more and more of His amazing grace through Jesus Christ? NO! (Romans 6:1-2, paraphrased). This means that we as believers must make a conscious choice and take a firm stand against sin, and the God of peace himself will make us *holy* (sanctify us) in every way—spirit, soul and body. Therefore, sin has no more power to condemn us, and God Himself will keep us blameless until our Lord Jesus Christ comes back. How do we know that this will happen? Because—*He who calls you is faithful to do it*! (1Thessalonians 5:24).

Write on the lines below any spirit-inspired thoughts or revelations concerning your personal tug-of-war with sin.

_____
_____
_____
_____
_____
_____
_____
_____
_____
_____
_____
_____
_____
_____

Time With God Prayer

Father God, help your children walk according to the spirit and not according to the flesh. Give us the spiritual endurance when things seem hard and the war within rages. Help us always to remember Christ is our anchor in this spiritual tug-a-war! It's in the omnipotent name of Jesus I pray. Amen.

Meditate on Romans 8:1. Write out on the lines below your personal prayer for sanctification. Ask God to cleanse you within so that you may live for him without.

_____
_____
_____
_____
_____
_____
_____
_____
_____
_____
_____
_____
_____
_____
_____
_____

In Jesus' name, I pray, Amen.

This page intentionally left blank.

Day Sixteen
Spiritual Physique

Do not conform to the pattern of this world, but be transformed by the renewing of your mind. Then you will be able to test and approve what God's will is—his good, pleasing and perfect will (Romans 12:2, NIV).

Oftentimes, there are vast differences between the measure of care we give to our "physical physique" (outer being) as opposed to the care we give to our "spiritual physique" (inner being). Therefore, many times, at the start of a new year, countless resolutions to "lose weight" are made, only to be abandoned by the time Valentine's Day rolls around.

If we are totally honest, what people think about *how* or *what* our outer appearance should look like carries a lot of weight (no pun intended) in today's society. So, at the beginning of each New Year, the mad rush to lose those pounds packed on during the holiday season begins. Thus, resolutions are earnestly made to do better, spend wiser, exercise regularly, and eat healthier. And the list goes on and on. Commitments are made to take better care of yourself overall—mentally and physically. So, you join a gym, take up yoga, revise your budget, and declare a 30-day detox.

Soon your physical body adjusts to the changes in your eating habits, and you notice that you no longer feel as many hunger pains as when you first started detoxing. You also notice that you have more energy, and it takes much less food than before to get that satisfied, full feeling. You begin to see welcomed changes in your physical physique. It's time to rejoice because your clothes now fit a little less snug, and you are so very proud of what you accomplished—*you look marvelous*!

But, what about your "*spiritual physique?*" Have you noticed any changes? Any differences in your "spiritual habits?" Are your motives, attitudes, actions and reactions becoming more *God*-pleasing rather than *self*-pleasing? Do you find yourself meditating on God's Word and His goodness more and more throughout the day? Do you *see* God's handiwork all around you in a different light? Do you see *God's hand* working in every area of your life—regardless of your circumstances? Do you feel His power, see His protection, and sense His presence moment-by-moment? Do you feel God's unconditional love embracing you throughout your day—counting IT ALL joy and a blessing? Do you feel His STRENGTH refreshing and renewing your soul, giving you the power for holy living that you need each day?

Well, pondering upon and sincerely answering this myriad of questions on a personal level will help you have better insight on what the Apostle Paul meant when he said, "*Do not conform any longer to the pattern of this world, but be transformed by the renewing of your mind*" (Romans 12:2, NIV). If you truly desire a lasting change in your *spiritual physique*—experiencing God at a deeper level, in His way, in His time, and in His power as you never have before—then commit to no longer "conforming" to the world's standards, which will require a new way of thinking (renewed mind) through Jesus Christ. As a result, believers will begin to have more influence on the world for Christ, rather than the world influencing believers for Satan.

A big part of undergoing this radical change in your

spiritual physique is to have a *mind* made up to live for Christ. Even the once-popular singing group "En Vogue" had it right when they sang, *"free your mind…and the rest will follow!"* Free your mind from worldly ways and surrender all to Christ—body, soul, and *mind*! As sinners saved by God's amazing grace, we must refocus our thoughts and renew our minds through the consistent washing of the *Word, Prayer* and *Praise* before any real transformation in our *lifestyle* can take place. *"Then you will be able to test and approve what God's will is—His good, pleasing and perfect will"* (Romans 12:2, NIV).

~*THINK ABOUT IT*~

If you think that this type of spiritual physique is impossible to attain based upon your past track record, then stop that "stinking thinking" and take a look at Philippians 4:8, which tells us how and what we should "think on" in order to renew our minds. *"Finally, brethren, whatever things are true, whatever things are noble, whatever things are just, whatever things are pure, whatever things are lovely, whatever things are of good report, if there is any virtue and if there is anything praiseworthy – meditate on these things."*

Write out on the lines below specific steps you will take to renew your mind and boost the spiritual transformation process to the new you. Then rejoice in what the Lord will do!

_____
_____
_____
_____
_____
_____
_____
_____
_____
_____
_____
_____
_____
_____
_____

Time With God Prayer

Father God, help your children release their minds to the cleansing power of the Holy Spirit, allowing Him to transform them into the spiritual newness of life you desire. It's in the transforming name of Jesus the Christ I pray. Amen.

Meditate on Philippians 4:8. Write out on the lines below your personal prayer for spiritual renewal and transformation through Christ Jesus.

_____
_____
_____
_____
_____
_____
_____
_____
_____
_____
_____
_____
_____
_____
_____
_____
_____
_____

In Jesus' name, I pray, Amen.

This page intentionally left blank.

Day Seventeen
Fear or Faith?

Be strong and courageous; do not be afraid nor dismayed before the king of Assyria, nor before all the multitude that is with him; for there are more with us than with him. With him is an arm of flesh; but with us is the LORD our God, to help us and to fight our battles." And the people were strengthened by the words of Hezekiah king of Judah (2 Chronicles 32:7-8).

When Hezekiah, king of Judah, saw that the Assyrians had come into Judah to make war against Jerusalem, he instructed the people to stop up all the springs and brooks that ran through the land as a tactic to discourage the Assyrians from conquering Jerusalem. Hezekiah also had the city wall that was broken rebuilt and raised, built another outside wall to fortify the city, and crafted a host of weapons and shields in preparation for battle. Then Hezekiah did something many leaders do when the people are on the brink of war, and things appear dismal.

He gathered the people together and gave them a pep talk saying, *"Be strong and courageous; do not be afraid nor dismayed before the king of Assyria, nor before all the multitude that is with him; for there are more with us than with him"* (2 Chronicles 32:7).

Fear—this is an emotion most of us have experienced at some time in our lives. It can come upon us gradually or suddenly. It can be experienced as a result of real or perceived danger, evil, pain, etc. It can be triggered due to a phobia or something one might dread or have trepidation concerning.

Regardless of the motive behind our fears, the Bible tells us on many occasions to *"fear not."* Well, that might seem easier said than done — especially when there is an imminent cause to be fearful staring you right in the face. This is the exact situation the people of Jerusalem and King Hezekiah found themselves in when the Assyrian army loomed outside their city walls.

Not only did the Assyrian army show up in massive numbers, Sennacherib, King of Assyria, also sent his servants ahead to Jerusalem to taunt the people, speak against their Lord God, and slander King Hezekiah. Sennacherib himself also spoke against God and even wrote letters to revile the Lord God of Israel. His soldiers constantly barracked the people of Jerusalem who were on the city wall in order to frighten them and scare them into submission so they might capture the city. This was psychological warfare at its best!

But none of the Assyrian tricks and fear tactics succeeded. Instead, King Hezekiah and the prophet, Isaiah, prayed and cried out to the Lord for help. In response to their fervent prayers of faith, the Lord God sent an angel to their rescue. Without Hezekiah or his army having to strike a single blow, the angel cut down every mighty man of valor, leader, and captain in the camp of the king of Assyria! To top that off, Sennacherib returned home shamefaced and disgraced. Then to add injury to insult, he was slaughtered by his own sons when he went into his god's temple (2 Chronicles 32:15-22).

Faith won out over fear! For King Hezekiah and the people of Jerusalem, it was a test of their faith not to succumb to their fears.

What are you afraid of? What causes you to worry? What keeps you awake at night? What scares you or causes you to panic instead of pray?

These questions may seem simple, but they are intended

to focus on your *fears*. However, like Hezekiah's pep talk to the people of Jerusalem, let's flip the mental switch for a moment and look at a set of different questions.

What gets you out of bed in the morning? What gives you hope? What gives you STRENGTH when you feel you can't go on? Now, these questions have a very different connotation, and they are intended to focus on the inspirational, motivational and spiritual aspects of life—*faith*.

The next time you are faced with *fear*—tap into your *faith*—pray and be encouraged through God's promises. Feed your faith, and your fears will fade! Remember the words of King Hezekiah. *"The Lord, your God, will help you and fight for you."* Jesus to the rescue!

~THINK ABOUT IT~

In order to be strong and courageous when facing imminent or perceived dangers, toils and snares, fear must be brought under control. After all, courage is not the absence of fear, but rather fear under control.

Therefore, when you find fear creeping in on you, remember this definition presented in the form of an acronym. F.E.A.R.—False Evidence Appearing Real. Then exercise your faith in the Lord your God by remembering that your Foundation is Anchored In Trusting HIM. Where is your F.A.I.T.H.?

Write your thoughts concerning faith and fear on the lines below.

_____
_____
_____
_____
_____
_____
_____
_____
_____
_____
_____
_____
_____
_____
_____
_____

Time With God Prayer

Father God, help your children release their fears into your capable hands, realizing that having you fight for us is more than the world fighting against us. It's in the strong and matchless name of Jesus the Christ I pray. Amen.

Meditate on Philippians 4:6-7. Write out on the lines below your personal prayer to release fear and exercise faith in all areas of your life.

_____
_____
_____
_____
_____
_____
_____
_____
_____
_____
_____
_____
_____
_____
_____
_____
_____
_____
_____

In Jesus' name, I pray, Amen.

This page intentionally left blank.

Day Eighteen
Lord, Make Me Over!

Now the Lord is the Spirit: and where the Spirit of the Lord is, there is liberty. But we all, with unveiled face beholding as in a mirror the glory of the Lord, are transformed into the same image from glory to glory, even as from the Lord the Spirit (2 Corinthians 3:17-18, ASV).

Pruning is a necessary process in the life of the believer. The very essence of the act of pruning involves clipping, cutting, trimming or peeling back the outer layer of an object, person or thing. The intent of pruning is to take away or separate the parts of that which is superfluous, undesired, or hinders growth and the fullness of beauty.

When God prunes his children, it is to help them grow spiritually strong and tall until they reflect the fullness of His glory! This is not a process that can be rushed.

Therefore, God takes the time needed as He carefully and skillfully, with great detail, slowly and strategically removes layers of our lives that cause a dull and distorted reflection of Him.

This pruning process may include the cutting away of some people, places and things in your life. Or perhaps the lopping off of some wrong attitudes, bad habits and horrible hang-ups. The Father carefully removes anything that keeps His children from looking like Christ and reflecting His glory.

Although the process may be painful, and the price of pruning may seem high while you are going through it, the end result will be spectacular!

"But we all, with unveiled face beholding as in a mirror the glory of the Lord, are transformed into the same image from glory to glory, even as from the Lord the Spirit" (2 Corinthians 3:18, ASV).

However, the process of obtaining *brokenness* is quite different. When something is broken, it is quickly and abruptly separated, shattered or destroyed. This state of brokenness can take place at any time in the life of a believer. Whether brought on by the actions of others or self-inflicted pain, agony or emotional distress, there is usually no time or steps taken to adjust to the change or ease the pain. Immediate severance takes place with no anesthesia.

Oftentimes, when brokenness occurs, there is no fight left in you. So with hands up in the air, you shout, "I give up!" But don't despair. The apostle Paul reminds us that even in a state of brokenness, although we may be cast down, we are never destroyed because of the powerful treasure we have deep within us — The Holy Spirit.

"But we have this treasure in earthen vessels that the excellence of the power may be of God and not of us. We are hard-pressed on every side, yet not crushed; we are perplexed, but not in despair; persecuted, but not forsaken; struck down, but not destroyed — always carrying about in the body the dying of the Lord Jesus, that the life of Jesus also may be manifested in our body" (2 Corinthians 4:7-10).

Pruning and brokenness — both have a place in the life of the believer. Both encompass a process unique to its own identity. And both are specifically designed to help us *walk in freedom* from the bondage of sin, STRENGTHEN *our resolve,* and *grow us* in God's grace as his precious children.

Are you willing to submit to the pruning process in order to glorify God and reach your fullest potential in Christ?

Pruning is painful but necessary.

Therefore, God has graciously given us His spirit to teach, correct and direct us through the process. Simply pray, *"Lord, make me over!"*

~THINK ABOUT IT~

The Lord is the Spirit who gives new life! With that new life comes liberty—freedom to live no longer bound by the laws of sin. Unveiled, believers can be mirrors that brilliantly reflect the glory of the Lord! This means that as the Spirit of the Lord works within you, you gradually and continuously shed away the "old you" as you become more and more (from glory to glory) like Christ. I'd rather be like Christ. What about you?

Think about the areas of your life that need "pruning" and write them down on the lines below.

_____
_____
_____
_____
_____
_____
_____
_____
_____
_____
_____
_____
_____
_____
_____
_____
_____

Time With God Prayer

Father God, help your children that are experiencing brokenness to realize that although cast down, they are still not destroyed, and therefore, by your grace, remain unconquered! Lord, help them realize that he who Christ sets free is free indeed — through Christ, we have the victory! It's in the victorious name of Jesus the Christ I pray. Amen.

Meditate on 2 Corinthians 3:17-18. Write out on the lines below your personal prayer to shed the ways of the world and become more like Christ.

_____
_____
_____
_____
_____
_____
_____
_____
_____
_____
_____
_____
_____
_____
_____
_____

In Jesus' name, I pray, Amen.

Day Nineteen
Armed & Dangerous

Finally, be strong in the Lord and in the strength of his might. Put on the whole armor of God, that you may be able to stand against the wiles of the devil. For we do not wrestle against flesh and blood, but against principalities, against powers, against the rulers of the darkness of this age, against spiritual hosts of wickedness in the heavenly places. Therefore, take up the whole armor of God, that you may be able to withstand in the evil day, and having done all, to stand. Stand therefore, having fastened on the belt of truth, and having put on the breastplate of righteousness, and, as shoes for your feet, having put on the readiness given by the gospel of peace. In all circumstances take up the shield of faith, with which you can extinguish all the flaming darts of the evil one; and take the helmet of salvation, and the sword of the spirit, which is the word of God. Praying at all times in the spirit, with all prayer and supplication. To that end, keep alert with all perseverance, making supplication for all the saints (Ephesians 6:10-18).

We are at war!

As a result, our future is resting on a fragile foundation. Day after day, Christians are losing ground to the enemy without it being very difficult to conquer. Why? Because believers continue the futile attempt to fight spiritual battles using carnal weapons. Yes—we are in spiritual warfare.

Make no mistake about it—from the moment you awake in the morning until the time you go to bed at night, and even while you slumber and sleep—there is a spiritual war raging!

This was the message the apostle Paul gave to the church

at Ephesus back then, and this very same message holds true for the church today. *We are in the middle of spiritual warfare.*

Paul warns the church that we wrestle not against flesh and blood, but against principalities, forces of evil, powers and wickedness in heavenly and high places. Against such as these, *worldly weapons won't work – it's a supernatural thang!*

Satan's mission remains the same today as it was in Paul's day – to kill, steal and destroy the believer by any means necessary. Satan has been on that mission for a very long time and has gotten very good at it. He never gives up, and he never quits. That old devil just don't play fair!

Satan is always looking for the believer's blindside or weak spot – that area in which you are most vulnerable. Then he attacks without warning or expectation. Yes, if the devil can't kill you, he will try to trick, trap and trip you up in your spiritual walk. This satanic tactic is used in order to render the believer powerless and ineffective as a Christian because Satan knows your soul is secure in Jesus and sealed until the day of redemption. In other words, you can't lose your salvation, but you can lose spiritual ground in this warfare.

Therefore, if Satan can cause the believer to lose spiritual ground in day-to-day battles all believers must fight – to walk in a dilemma instead of deliverance or live in defeat instead of walk in victory – then mission accomplished!

Thus, Paul gives the church some most vital and valuable advice on how to defeat the enemy and walk in victory – take up and put on the whole Armor of God that you may be able to stand in that evil day!

Paul's battle plan for the believer to be victorious in that "evil day" – during the most intense moments of satanic attacks, temptations, crisis or tragedy – is to always be *battle-ready* and *dressed to kill* the enemy. Therefore, as a believer, when it comes to facing and resisting the infernal enemy,

Satan, always remember:
- You cannot fight spiritual battles with carnal weapons.
- Your armor is specifically designed to protect and defend you from danger and attacks of the enemy.
- Your armor is your "spiritual identify" in Christ — *never take it off.*
- Your best defense and offense against Satan's attacks is to always be *battle-ready* and *praying in the spirit.*

Each day before you leave home in the morning, don't forget to look into the spiritual mirror of *Ephesians 6* to make sure you have your *war clothes on* and are strategically *dressed to kill* the enemy!

~THINK ABOUT IT~

Ephesians Chapter 6 lists six pieces of the Whole Armor of God. In verse 18, it includes the significant role of prayer in this spiritual warfare. Below are short examples of how each of these elements should translate or look in the life of a believer in order to be protected from the dangerous darts of the devil. On the lines below, identify your strengths and weaknesses (growth areas) for each spiritual element.

1. **Belt of Truth** — Integrity (Honesty, respect, trust)

_____

_____

_____

2. **Breastplate of Righteousness** — Transparency (Purity of heart is required.

_____

_____

_____

3. **Shoes for Feet** — Tranquility (Walk in the Word — Gospel of Peace)

_____

_____

_____

4. **Shield of Faith** — Certainty (Confidence in God)

_____
_____
_____
_____

5. **Helmet of Salvation** — Protection (Guarding your head, ears and eye gates from all the insanity of the world)

_____
_____
_____
_____

6. **Sword of the Spirit** — Word of God (Hide God's word in your heart)

_____
_____
_____
_____

7. **Pray in the Spirit** — Practice Holy alertness (Learn to pray all kinds of prayers to combat the enemy and grow spiritually strong for the battle)

_____
_____
_____
_____
_____

Time With God Prayer

Father God, thank you that the victory is ours, and we can trust you to fight our battles. Help us also understand that we still must show up for the fight — battle ready! It's in the matchless name of Jesus the Christ I pray. Amen.

Meditate on Ephesians 6:10-18. Write out on the lines below your personal prayer to grow stronger in the areas of weakness previously identified. Praise God for your areas of STRENGTH that you might continue to glorify His name even the more.

_____
_____
_____
_____
_____
_____
_____
_____
_____
_____
_____
_____
_____
_____
_____
_____
_____

In Jesus' name, I pray, Amen.

Day Twenty
The Belly of the Beast

Now the LORD had prepared a great fish to swallow Jonah. And Jonah was in the belly of the fish three days and three nights (Jonah 1:17).

You may have heard the story of Jonah and the whale. This was one of my favorite Bible stories as a child because it was full of adventure and the wonders of God. Just to think about a man living inside the belly of a whale for three days and nights stirred my imagination. Not to mention the whale vomiting him up on dry land—and he survived!

Yes, Jonah endured some hardships while in the belly of the whale, but it was all because of his own doing. Although captivating, Jonah's story was about much more than adventure. If you look closely at chapters 1-4 in the book of Jonah, you will see that this is actually a tale of a man's disobedience, judgment, unforgiveness and lack of mercy and compassion. At the same time, the story displays God's patience, mercy, love, compassion, forgiveness, provision, deliverance and sovereignty.

You see, God knows just what it will take for each one of His children to realize their wicked ways, repent, and turn back to Him. This is why God instructed Jonah to go down to Nineveh and preach to the people there who were blinded by sin and ignorant to God's pending judgment. But Jonah, having first-hand knowledge and experience with God's grace, compassion and lovingkindness towards those who repent, could only see his selfish reasoning for disobedience to God and lack of compassion towards the people of Nineveh. Blinded by personal anger, Jonah opted to die rather than see Nineveh spared!

"But it greatly displeased Jonah and he became angry. He prayed to the LORD and said, "O LORD, is this not what I said when I was still in my country? That is why I ran to Tarshish, because I knew that You are a gracious and compassionate God, slow to anger and great in lovingkindness, and [when sinners turn to You], You revoke the [sentence of] disaster [against them]. Therefore now, O LORD, just take my life from me, for it is better for me to die than to live." Then the LORD said, "Do you have a good reason to be angry?" Then Jonah went out of the city and sat east of it. There he made himself a shelter and sat under its shade so that he could see what would happen in the city" (Jonah 4:1-5, AMP).

God had to teach Jonah a lesson in love, mercy, grace, forgiveness and compassion for others the hard way. But, at Jonah's expense, believers today can learn some very valuable lessons taken from his journey through *"the belly of the beast."*

~THINK ABOUT IT~

Below are four vital lessons to remember when you find yourself in a potentially fatal fix!

1. **Get Comfortable** — because you may be in that place for a while. Think about "how" you got in that mess in the first place. Then confess, repent, and obey without delay.
2. **Learn the Lesson Being Taught** — or else you just might have to repeat it again and again until you get it right.
3. **Trust God for Deliverance** — no matter how difficult the situation, God is able to deliver you out of all of your troubles — right on time.
4. **Pray, Praise and Obey** — this is always the best way out. Not only will you be delivered, but those who will hear and receive your testimony will be encouraged and blessed too.

Think about some sticky situations you've gotten into in the past and how you handled them. Now, think about the previous four lessons learned from Jonah's experience and how you could have applied them to achieve a more successful outcome. Write your thoughts on the lines below.

_____
_____
_____
_____
_____
_____
_____

Time With God Prayer

Father God, thank you for being loving, kind, merciful, compassionate and slow to anger. Help your children exemplify your character traits as we encounter others who are lost and blinded by worldly ways and sin. It's in the name of Jesus, the sovereign Savior, I pray. Amen.

Meditate on Jonah 2:1-9. If you are in a dilemma right now, pray to God like Jonah – confess and repent of your specific sins, ask God for deliverance, and then thank Him for His goodness and mercy towards you. Journal your personal prayer on the lines below.

_____
_____
_____
_____
_____
_____
_____
_____
_____
_____
_____
_____
_____
_____
_____
_____

In Jesus' name, I pray, Amen.

This page intentionally left blank.

Day Twenty-one
STRENGTH for the Believer

No temptation has overtaken you but such as is common to man; and God is faithful, who will not allow you to be tempted beyond what you are able, but with the temptation will provide the way of escape also, so that you will be able to endure it (I Corinthians 10:13, NASB).

In a previous devotion, I shared with you that in today's society, almost everyone is hung-up on how they look. Our physical appearance is very important to us — at least to most of us. We invest countless amounts of our time, energy and money just so we can *"look good."* Some even go to extreme measures to get that *"physical physique"* (outward appearance) they desire to have.

But what about your *"spiritual physique"* (inner being) that God desires his children to have? What drastic changes or extreme makeovers are you willing to undergo in order to STRENGTHEN your inner being, so when the storms, trials, and tribulations of life come (and they will come), you will be able to STAND and ENDURE?

The Bible says, *"No temptation"* (regardless of its source) that will come upon (overtake or entice) the believer that is not *"common to man"* (known to the human experience) or beyond human resistance — but along with the temptation, God will always provide *"the way out"* as well, so that you *"will be able to endure it"* (without yielding), and you will, therefore, be able to overcome the temptation (I Corinthians

10:13, Paraphrased with parts from AMP).

This scripture is often misunderstood by believers to think God will never allow any strong temptations to cross our paths, and if He does, there will immediately be "a way to escape" so we will not have to "endure" any hardships, trials, sufferings, troubles or pain. Therefore, when these situations land at our front door, we immediately begin to search for another "way out."

However, this scripture actually means that no temptation, trial or sin—no matter what form it appears or how it may attempt to lead you astray—is beyond human resistance. Why? Because God is faithful to His Word and character. Therefore, He will adjust or adapt the "temptation" (sent by the enemy, not by God) to fit the human experience so you may be able to *endure it*—physically, mentally and spiritually.

Remember the story of Job? *"Then the LORD said to Satan, "Have you considered My servant Job, that there is none like him on the earth, a blameless and upright man, one who fears God and shuns evil? And still he holds fast to his integrity, although you incited Me against him, to destroy him without cause." So Satan answered the LORD and said, "Skin for skin! Yes, all that a man has he will give for his life. But stretch out Your hand now, and touch his bone and his flesh, and he will surely curse You to Your face!" And the LORD said to Satan, "Behold, he is in your hand, but spare his life"* (Job 2:3-6).

Think about it this way—perhaps your "way out" is "*through endurance.*" Job endured many losses—cattle, children, property, friends and even his health was not safe from the enemy's attack. And although his wife lived, he lost her confidence in his faithfulness to God. Everything of value Job had was gone. Nevertheless, his victory came through his endurance—not escape!

"And the LORD restored Job's losses when he prayed for his friends. Indeed the LORD gave Job twice as much as he had before. Then all his brothers, all his sisters, and all those who had been his acquaintances before, came to him and ate food with him in his house; and they consoled him and comforted him for all the adversity that the LORD had brought upon him. Each one gave him a piece of silver and each a ring of gold. Now the LORD blessed the latter days of Job more than his beginning; for he had fourteen thousand sheep, six thousand camels, one thousand yoke of oxen, and one thousand female donkeys. He also had seven sons and three daughters...In all the land were found no women so beautiful as the daughters of Job; and their father gave them an inheritance among their brothers. After this Job lived one hundred and forty years, and saw his children and grandchildren for four generations. So Job died, old and full of days" (Job 42:10-17).

God never promised that the Christian life would be easy. Matter of fact, the Bible tells us we *will endure* tribulations, but to be of good cheer. The believer can still experience the "peace of God" as you *"go through"* what you are trying to get through.

"These things I have spoken to you, that in Me you may have peace. In the world you will have tribulation; but be of good cheer, I have overcome the world" (John 16:33).

Child of God, although at times in your life (perhaps even right now) you may have to *walk through the valley* and the shadow of death, God is faithful to keep His promise to never leave or forsake you (see Psalm 23). God, Himself will be your refuge and STRENGTH, a very present help in times of trouble (see Psalm 46:1). Therefore, no matter what you must endure, God will be right there with you—leading, guiding, directing, protecting, holding and STRENGTHENING you every step of the way.

YOUR NAME IS VICTORY!

~THINK ABOUT IT~

If you've been wondering how you're going to *"get through, what you are going through,"* then try taking God at His Word and launch out into the deep waters of FAITH. The biggest fish are caught in the deepest waters, so step out into the deep waters of your faith and watch the abundant blessings of the Lord overflow!

Write on the lines below those things you need to trust God with. Then totally surrender them to Him, withholding nothing!

_____
_____
_____
_____
_____
_____
_____
_____
_____
_____
_____
_____
_____
_____
_____
_____
_____
_____
_____

Time With God Prayer

Father God, help your children realize that we are all in need of a spiritual makeover! Point out the places in our lives that need your loving touch and help us release them into your capable hands. Father, you are the potter, and we are the clay. Mold us, shape us and make us over until we reflect your glory! It's in the name of Jesus I pray. Amen.

Meditate on Psalm 23. Write out on the lines below your personal prayer for physical, emotional and spiritual STRENGTH to get through what you are going through.

_____
_____
_____
_____
_____
_____
_____
_____
_____
_____
_____
_____
_____
_____
_____

In Jesus' name, I pray, Amen.

ABOUT THE AUTHOR

Mary A. Ford
Author * Speaker * Teacher * Prayer Leader
For Booking Information Contact Mary @ maford1958@gmail.com
or www.duty2delightministries.com

Mary is a native Texan and a resident of Arlington, Texas. Married to Reverend James A. Ford, Jr., they both serve in ministry together at the Koinonia Christian Church of Arlington, Texas, where she serves as the Prayer Ministry Director.

Mary is not only a PRAYER WARRIOR and PRAYER LEADER, she is also a TEACHER of God's WORD, having taught various classes and workshops on scripture-based prayer for over 20 years. She has received many awards and commendations in recognition of her faithfulness and Christian service. She has served as a presenter, session speaker and prayer leader for various marriage conferences, women's conferences, prayer breakfasts and prayer revivals. Together with her husband, Mary has conducted workshops on "Intimacy and Oneness" and "Praying Together to Stay Together" as a husband-wife team.

Whether FACILITATING a workshop, TEACHING a class, SPEAKING at a conference or conducting THE PRAYER FUELING STATION, Mary expels fervor, passion, enthusiasm, and conviction while moving audiences to embrace change through being hearers and doers. She captivates her audience while moving them to bring about positive, life-altering results in their lives.

Mary's workshops, sessions and classes on prayer have been described as *Interactive, Engaging, Motivational, Encouraging,* and *Life-changing.* Participants leave equipped and encouraged to truly seek a more intimate relationship with God through prayer—thus moving their prayer life "From Duty to Delight!"

Other Books by Mary A. Ford

From Duty to Delight: Are You Enjoying Jesus Yet?

A scripture-based weekly encouragement devotional divinely designed to inspire spiritual growth, uplift your spirit, strengthen your resolve, and encourage a transformed walk with Christ!

Hour of Power:
Moving Your Prayer Life to the Next Level

This book encourages Christians to cultivate a more powerful, purposeful and effective prayer life through spending dedicated, consistent, intimate time with the lover of their souls—and truly enjoy it!

Prayer: The Key to Unlocking Blessings—
12 Days of Prayer & Fasting

This devotional-style book contains 12 specific scripture-based Prayer Focuses—one for each of the 12 Days of Prayer and Fasting. Each prayer focus contains several Prayer Points to guide you through your personal prayer time and throughout the day. It also includes dedicated pages to journal your personal prayers and capture spiritual insights for specific needs—all based on the prayer focus of the day. Sample prayers included for each day encourage you along the way.

* All books available online at Amazon.com and through other retailers.

Mary's Most Popular Prayer Classes and Workshops

Book Mary A. Ford Online
www.duty2delightministries.com

Hour of Power: Moving Your Prayer Life to the Next Level

An eight-week scripture-based prayer curriculum designed to better equip Christians who have a desire to enhance their personal prayer life and pray more effectively. Participants will be challenged to:
- Make prayer a priority in their lives
- Develop consistency in their prayer lives
- Learn to master various prayer elements
- Increase their personal prayer time with God

Prayer That Works

An eight-week scripture-based prayer curriculum that takes you on a journey through the powerful prayer life of the Old Testament Prophet, Elijah.

This course is designed to DEVELOP, STRENGTHEN and ENHANCE the believer's personal relationship with God through the power of prayer. Participants will be challenged to:
- Make prayer a priority through increased personal time with God
- Develop intimacy with God through consistency in prayer
- Strengthen personal commitment to God through accountability and prayer partners
- Develop an effective prayer life — praying effectual, fervent *Prayers That Work*

Prayer Boot Camp 101

Learn to master the prayer basics through this 90-minute, power-packed prayer workshop. Participants will learn:
- What prayer is
- What prayer does
- What hinders prayer
- What effective prayer requires
- How to get started—developing an effective prayer plan

Praying Together to Stay Together

In this 90-minute marriage workshop, participants will learn the power of prayer in marriage and True ONENESS! Participants will learn:
- How prayer deepens our relationship with God and one another
- How prayer naturally brings couples into agreement with one another
- How to go before the Lord with our concerns in unity of heart, mind, and spirit

Prayer: A Prelude to Worship

This 90-minute workshop is designed to take your music ministry and praise team to the next level through the power of prayer and worship! Workshop goals and objectives:
- Reveal the powerful connection that Christians have with God through Prayer
- Explore the significance of prayer in worship
- See how prayer impacts personal and corporate praise and worship

This page intentionally left blank.